Original title:
Where I Belong

Copyright © 2024 Swan Charm
All rights reserved.

Author: Linda Leevike
ISBN HARDBACK: 978-9916-89-676-1
ISBN PAPERBACK: 978-9916-89-677-8
ISBN EBOOK: 978-9916-89-678-5

## Between Shadows and Light

In the stillness, whispers reside,
Hearts yearning for truth, we confide.
Stars shimmer softly, guiding our way,
Through valleys of night, into the day.

Each moment we seek, a glimpse of grace,
Hand in hand, we find our place.
In shadows, He guides with gentle might,
Leading us forward, embracing the light.

With faith as our beacon, we rise above,
Echoing tales of eternal love.
In the dance of the dusk, a promise unfurls,
Where shadows embrace the light of the world.

## **Echoes of the Divine**

In silence, a voice softly calls,
A melody echoes through temple walls.
Fingers of time weave threads of the past,
Bringing forth wisdom, a truth unsurpassed.

The mountains stand tall, witnesses so grand,
In the stillness we feel the Creator's hand.
Every prayer whispered, a sacred thread,
In the tapestry woven, our spirits are fed.

Under the heavens, we gather in peace,
In unity's arms, our burdens release.
Each heartbeat a hymn, rising above,
In the echoes of the Divine, we find love.

## A Sacred Path Awaits

Upon the horizon, where dawn breaks anew,
A sacred path, drawing hearts true.
Each step we take, guided by faith,
In the presence of grace, we find our place.

Through meadows of hope, we wander free,
With every breath, a prayer to be.
Holding the light of the generations,
In joy and in sorrow, lifelong relations.

The sun paints a canvas of dreams in the sky,
Our spirits ascend, like birds we fly.
With love as our compass, forever we chase,
A sacred path awaits, our souls embrace.

## The Chorus of Kindred Spirits

In the gathering dusk, our voices entwine,
A chorus of kindred, in sacred design.
Each note a whisper, a story to share,
Together in harmony, hearts laid bare.

With laughter, we resonate, joy in the air,
Trusting the bond that we willingly bear.
Through trials and triumphs, together we stand,
Hand in hand, we walk, across this vast land.

In life's great theatre, all roles intertwine,
Each spirit a star, together we shine.
The chorus of kindred, a melody sweet,
In unity's anthem, our hearts find their beat.

## Sanctuary of the Heart

In silence deep, the spirit sings,
A haven found, where love still clings.
Within the shadows, grace unfolds,
A sacred warmth, the heart beholds.

In prayerful breath, the world subsides,
With every tear, redemption rides.
Each whispered vow, a soft refrain,
In this sanctuary, peace remains.

Amidst the trials, faith will rise,
Through every doubt, the heart still flies.
A sacred space where souls unite,
Transcending darkness, embracing light.

With faith as light, the path made clear,
Through every joy, through every fear.
A refuge found in love's embrace,
In the sanctuary, timeless grace.

## Home Among the Stars

Beneath the vast and starry dome,
We seek the light that guides us home.
In every blink, a promise glows,
Among the stars, our spirit knows.

With every wish cast to the night,
We reach for hope, embrace the light.
In cosmic arms, we are set free,
A celestial dance, eternity.

The heavens sing, a lullaby,
In astral touch, we learn to fly.
Each twinkling star, a spark divine,
In this vast space, our hearts entwine.

As galaxies twirl, we find our place,
In cosmic grace, a warm embrace.
Together bound, through time and space,
Home among the stars, in love we trace.

## **Whispers in Sacred Spaces**

In quiet corners, secrets dwell,
Where every heartbeat tells a tale.
In sacred spaces, time stands still,
With every breath, the world we fill.

The walls absorb each prayerful sound,
In whispered hopes, redemption found.
Through gentle light, the spirit soars,
In sacred spaces, love restores.

As shadows dance, the soul awakes,
In stillness deep, creation shakes.
Each fleeting moment, a chance to grow,
In whispers soft, our spirits flow.

With every sigh, new paths begun,
In sacred air, we are as one.
Together shared, a sacred trust,
In silent reverence, love is just.

## The Pilgrim's Embrace

Upon the road, the weary tread,
With faith as guide, by grace we're led.
In every step, a story blooms,
The pilgrim's heart, a path assumes.

Through valleys low and mountains high,
In seeking truth, we learn to fly.
With open arms, the journey calls,
In every rise, in every fall.

The road unfolds, a sacred quest,
With every trial, we find our rest.
In unity's light, our spirits weave,
In the pilgrim's embrace, we believe.

As dawn breaks forth, a new refrain,
Through every joy, through every pain,
We walk together, hand in hand,
In the pilgrim's embrace, we understand.

## The Heart's Tabernacle

In the quiet of the soul's retreat,
Whispers of grace and mercy meet.
Sanctuary built on faith's embrace,
Where love and hope find their place.

A prayerful heart, a sacred space,
Echoes of joy, a warmest trace.
With every beat, divine unfolds,
Stories of peace and truth retold.

In shadows cast, His light shall shine,
Each thought and deed, a love divine.
The heart, a vessel, pure and bright,
Guided by faith, embracing light.

In silence deep, the spirit's call,
Reminds us gently we are all.
Beloved children, hand in hand,
Together in this promised land.

And when the night draws close in fight,
We lift our eyes to seek His light.
For in this heart's tabernacle true,
His presence always shines anew.

## A Journey into the Sacred

Step by step, the path unfolds,
In sacred whispers, stories told.
With every breath, the spirit sings,
Of love that soars on timeless wings.

Through winding trails, our souls will roam,
In nature's arms, we find our home.
Each moment blessed, a treasure rare,
A journey graced by fervent prayer.

The mountains rise, the rivers flow,
In every grain, His wonders show.
In fleeting time, His truth we'll find,
Guiding us gently, heart and mind.

The stars above, a cosmic guide,
Illuminate the love inside.
As we walk onward, hand in hand,
In unity, we take our stand.

With open hearts, we seek the light,
A journey borne of faith and sight.
In every step, divine will flow,
To lands of peace where blessings grow.

## Within the Arms of Affection

In tender moments, love reveals,
A gentle touch, the heart it heals.
Within the arms of pure embrace,
We find our strength, our sacred space.

In laughter shared and tears that flow,
Compassion blooms, a radiant glow.
A balm for wounds, both deep and sore,
In every hug, we're cherished more.

The bonds we weave, with threads of grace,
Hold us together, time can't erase.
In every smile, a spark ignites,
The fire of love that warms the nights.

In trials faced, we're never alone,
Together, a strength we've grown.
With hearts entwined, we rise above,
United always, bound by love.

So let us gather, hearts in tune,
Within the arms of love, we bloom.
In every heartbeat, our truth is clear,
In affection's glow, we hold what's dear.

## The Light That Guides Us Home

In every shadow, hope will gleam,
A guiding star, a faithful dream.
The light that shines, both pure and bright,
Leads us onward through darkest night.

With every step, we trust the way,
Each dawn brings forth a brand new day.
In valleys low and mountains high,
His love will always be nearby.

Through trials faced and storms that rage,
The light of faith, our sacred page.
With courage drawn from His embrace,
We find our path, we run the race.

In every heart, a flame ignites,
Illuminating darkest nights.
Together, as we walk this road,
The light will guide us, share the load.

So fear not, dear soul, for you are known,
In every moment, love has grown.
With steadfast hearts, we journey on,
The light that guides us leads to dawn.

## Celestial Anchors

In the quiet night sky, stars align,
Guiding weary hearts through darkened times.
Their radiant glow, a promise divine,
A tether to hope, in love's gentle chimes.

Each prayer a beacon, reaching above,
To realms where compassion endlessly flows.
In faith, we find strength, anchored by love,
A sanctuary of trust, where joy grows.

Through trials we walk, with courage bestowed,
The path illuminated by sacred grace.
Together we share, this light on our road,
As the heavens embrace, in a warm embrace.

Celestial whispers, soft as a sigh,
Remind us of truths, forever embraced.
In the arms of the cosmos, we'll fly,
Bound by the love, that never shall waste.

So, let us soar high, on wings of belief,
With souls intertwined, our spirits ignite.
In the dance of the stars, find sweet relief,
For faith is our anchor, shining so bright.

## The Abode of Tranquility

In a garden where silence blooms so pure,
Whispers of solace fill the gentle air.
A haven of peace, where hearts endure,
Sheltering dreams wrapped in heavenly care.

The rustling leaves sing of timeless grace,
Each petal a prayer, soft and sincere.
Here, the spirit finds its sacred space,
In the stillness, love's promise draws near.

Underneath the vast sky's loving gaze,
We gather our thoughts, our worries laid bare.
In the glow of dawn, through mornings we praise,
For the blessings of life, our burdens to share.

In this abode, where hope flows like streams,
We echo the truth that time cannot sever.
With faith as our guide, we scatter our dreams,
In unity's warmth, we are now forever.

So let us abide, in this tranquil land,
With hearts intertwined, and faith intertwined.
Together we stand, hand in loving hand,
Fostering peace that transcends space and time.

## Journeying Through Faith

Steps carved in promise, each moment we tread,
Guided by whispers of the Divine light.
Through valleys of doubt, where shadows are spread,
We march on together, hearts tethered tight.

In the trials we face, our spirits unite,
Carried by voices that echo above.
In the darkest of nights, the stars shine so bright,
Reminders of grace and unconditional love.

Through winding paths, with courage we stride,
Each footfall a testament of dreams shared.
With faith as our compass, hope as our guide,
We forge on through storms, unafraid and prepared.

Every encounter, a chance to be blessed,
In the tapestry woven with threads of gold.
The love that we share, a sacred quest,
An unending journey, forever retold.

So with open hearts, we embrace the unknown,
Each lesson we learn, a stepping stone grand.
In the journey of faith, we are never alone,
Together we rise, through life's gentle hand.

## The Divine Mosaic

In the grand tapestry of life we weave,
Colors of kindness dance with grace divine.
Every soul a thread, together we cleave,
Creating a vision, a brilliant design.

Each story told, a beautiful page,
Reflecting the light that shines from within.
In unity's art, let us break the cage,
Forging bonds of love, where all can begin.

Fragments of hope spark the brightest glow,
In every embrace, compassion extends.
Through trials that come, our spirits will grow,
In the mosaic of life, where love transcends.

Every heartbeat sings a sacred refrain,
Binding us closer, through joy and through pain.
In the dance of our faith, we are one in the rain,
Finding strength in our hearts, as we softly explain.

So let us unite, hand in hand we shall stand,
Painting our lives with the hues of the sun.
In the masterpiece born from love's gentle hand,
We are all part of God's work, beautifully done.

## The Home of Heavenly Hues

In realms where light and purpose meet,
The whispers of dawn, serene and sweet.
A canvas painted with grace untold,
In every shade, a story unfolds.

The skies embrace the gentle night,
Bringing forth stars, pure and bright.
Each twinkle a promise, a dream to chase,
In the home of colors, we find our place.

Mountains rise with voices so grand,
Calling us forth to understand.
The rivers flow with a sacred tune,
Guiding our hearts like a soft monsoon.

In every corner, love's echo rings,
Nature speaks, and our spirit sings.
With every breath, we find anew,
The warmth and beauty in heavenly hues.

So let us gather beneath the skies,
With open hearts and longing eyes.
In the embrace of love's divine grace,
We find ourselves in this holy space.

## Shelter of the Seraphim

In shadows deep where angels dwell,
A refuge found, a timeless well.
With wings of light, they guard the way,
In the shelter of love, we long to stay.

The whispers soft, a guiding hand,
In every heartbeat, a sacred band.
In their presence, fear takes flight,
As they lead us to the dawn's pure light.

A sanctuary where hope is sown,
In quietude, the heart has grown.
Each prayer uplifted, a gentle song,
In the arms of angels, we all belong.

Beneath the stars, in the stillness bright,
The seraphim watch throughout the night.
Their love encircles, a warm embrace,
In every moment, we seek their grace.

So let us rest in this holy keep,
In the shelter of love, our souls to steep.
With faith aflame, we walk the path,
In union with the angels' wrath.

## Finding My Sacred Place

In the quiet glade where the wildflowers bloom,
I seek a moment devoid of gloom.
The rustling leaves, a gentle song,
In nature's arms, I feel I belong.

With every breath, the spirit sighs,
In the warm embrace of the endless skies.
A sacred space where the heart can race,
In the stillness, I find my grace.

The sunlit path beckons ahead,
Where thoughts of worry are softly shed.
In the dance of light, I learn to see,
The essence of love, cradling me.

With open arms, I welcome the day,
In sacred beauty, I find my way.
Where silence speaks, and hearts connect,
In the depth of stillness, I learn to reflect.

For in this space, I hear the call,
Of wisdom ancient, uniting us all.
Finding my place in life's sweet chase,
I gather strength in my sacred space.

## The Choir of Connected Hearts

In harmony, we gather near,
Voices rising, a song sincere.
Each note a bridge, a hand to hold,
In the choir of hearts, our love unfolds.

With laughter sweet and tears embraced,
Every joy shared, a life interlaced.
In melodies woven, we stand as one,
Under the blessings of moon and sun.

Resonating with the pulse of light,
We find our courage in the night.
In every heartbeat, the truth we find,
Connected souls, forever entwined.

Through trials faced and sorrows shared,
With open minds, we show we care.
In the rhythm of kindness, we rise above,
In the symphony of life, we share our love.

So let our voices blend and soar,
Knowing together, we are so much more.
In the choir of hearts, we shall remain,
A testament to joy, a balm for pain.

## **Threads of the Divine Fabric**

In the loom of faith we weave,
Threads of love, we believe.
Colors bright and shadows slight,
Crafting grace in morning light.

Each stitch a prayer, softly sewn,
Binding hearts, never alone.
Together we rise, as one we stand,
In the tapestry designed by His hand.

Through storms of doubt, we hold fast,
The fabric forged, from first to last.
In every tear, a lesson learned,
In every joy, a heart that yearned.

Threads of mercy gently spin,
The sacred dance where hope begins.
In unity, our spirits soar,
The divine fabric, forevermore.

The hand that guides, the heart that feels,
In every thread, the truth reveals.
Eternal patterns, woven tight,
Threads of the divine, our endless light.

## Atonement in Abundance

In shadows deep, we seek the way,
Atonement flows, a brightening ray.
With humble hearts and open hands,
We find peace where mercy stands.

Each misstep met with gentle grace,
Forgiveness blooms in a sacred space.
The burdens lifted, spirits free,
Atonement brings serenity.

Voices raised in hymns of praise,
Counting blessings through all our days.
With every tear, a grace bestowed,
The path to wholeness gently showed.

In the well of love, we drink deep,
Atonement's promise, our souls to keep.
With every act of kindness shared,
Abundance found where hearts have bared.

Embracing flaws, we grow anew,
In this journey, His love rings true.
For in our failures, we are found,
Atonement in abundance all around.

## The Refuge of the Redeemed

In the quiet, we find our peace,
A refuge granted, sweet release.
In gentle whispers, His voice calls,
Guiding us through life's great halls.

The lost and weary gather near,
In His embrace, we shed our fear.
With open arms, He holds us tight,
A beacon shining through the night.

The world may falter, shadows creep,
Yet in His love, our hearts will leap.
In every trial, we find our way,
The refuge of the redeemed we pray.

Through valleys low and mountains high,
We walk in faith, our spirits fly.
Each step a testament to grace,
In His haven, we find our place.

Together we sing, a sacred song,
In the refuge where we belong.
For in His care, forever sealed,
The Redeemed, in love, revealed.

## Pathways of Purpose

Upon the road, we seek the light,
Pathways of purpose, shining bright.
With every step, a call to serve,
In love and faith, we shall preserve.

The winding ways, not always clear,
Yet in His presence, we draw near.
With open hearts and eyes to see,
The path unfolds, His will to be.

Through trials faced, we find our might,
In every challenge, the test of sight.
Each purpose found, a gift to share,
To spread His light, beyond compare.

In unity, we walk as one,
With hope and love, our race begun.
In every moment, guidance sweet,
Pathways of purpose, our lives complete.

So let us walk in faith so true,
With every heartbeat, we renew.
In His embrace, we find our way,
Pathways of purpose lead to stay.

## Harmony in the Holy

In the silence of the dawn, we pray,
Hearts united, come what may.
Whispers of love fill the air,
Beneath the grace of hands that share.

Gentle souls in sacred choir,
Voices rise, we lift them higher.
With every note, the spirit soars,
Embraced by peace, forever yours.

In the garden where faith blooms,
Hope awakens, dispelling glooms.
Together we walk this holy ground,
In harmony, our souls are found.

The stars above sing of light,
Guiding us through the darkest night.
In every prayer, a bond we weave,
In love's embrace, we truly believe.

So let the world hear our song,
In unity, we all belong.
Chasing shadows with bright devotion,
In harmony, we find our motion.

## **Veil of Serenity**

Beneath the stillness, calm resides,
Where whispers linger, grace abides.
In every heart, a gentle sigh,
A veil of peace, it draws us nigh.

With eyes closed tight, we seek the light,
In moments pure, our spirits ignite.
Each breath a prayer, so softly said,
Where silence reigns, and sorrows shed.

Under azure skies, we find our way,
Guided by faith, come what may.
In the stillness, our souls embrace,
Wrapped in love, a sweet solace.

Let go of burdens, let spirit flow,
In the quiet, we come to know.
From every tear, a pearl is made,
In seraphic light, our fears will fade.

So in this realm, with hearts exposed,
We gather strength as light bestowed.
Veiled in serenity, we stand tall,
In the embrace of love, we find it all.

## The Oasis of Faith

In the desert of doubt, we seek the stream,
A cool refuge, a holy dream.
Where hope glimmers like a star,
In the oasis, we wander far.

With each step, the spirit flows,
Through barren lands, where courage grows.
In shadows cast by troubled skies,
Faith illuminates, and never dies.

A chalice raised, we share our plight,
In unity, we find our might.
With whispers soft, we call His name,
In the oasis, our hearts aflame.

The palm trees sway, a gentle breeze,
In sacred moments, our souls find ease.
The water's edge, where blessings pour,
In every drop, we seek for more.

So let us gather by the well,
In stories told, our spirits swell.
In the oasis, forever we stay,
In faith's embrace, we find our way.

## Lighthouse of the Weary

Amidst the storm, a beacon shines,
A guiding light through testing times.
In shadows deep, we find our way,
The lighthouse stands, night turns to day.

Waves may crash with fervent might,
But in His glow, we sense the light.
With heavy hearts, we climb the stair,
To find our solace, His loving care.

The tides may pull with bitter force,
But love's embrace will chart our course.
In every trial, a lesson learned,
Through darkest hours, the flame still burns.

So raise your eyes where hope resides,
In faith's embrace, our spirit glides.
Through tempests fierce, we hold on tight,
Trusting in the lighthouse's light.

Together we stand, the weary and worn,
With hearts united, reborn.
In the harbor of grace, we find our peace,
The lighthouse of love will never cease.

## Woven in Holy Light

In shadows cast, your love will shine,
A guiding hand through darkened times,
Each thread of faith, a design divine,
We walk together, hearts as chimes.

The sacred text, a whispered prayer,
In moments still, we find our way,
With every breath, your presence near,
In woven light, our souls shall stay.

The stars above, a sacred choir,
Singing hymns of peace and grace,
Through trials faced, we rise higher,
In holy love, we find our place.

With every dawn, a promise new,
Your mercy flows like morning dew,
In unity, our spirits grew,
Woven in light, our faith is true.

## In the Embrace of Grace

In quiet fields where lilies grow,
Your gentle touch, a soft caress,
Through whispered winds, your love does flow,
In the embrace of grace, we find rest.

With outstretched arms, you welcome all,
Each heart a vessel meant to hold,
In every rise, in every fall,
Your hand, a guide, forever bold.

The rivers sing with joyful praise,
Reflecting life in harmony,
Through every trial, your light stays,
In grace's arms, we are set free.

Through storms and strife, we walk as one,
In faith we grow, in light we stand,
In the embrace of love begun,
Together, guided by your hand.

## **Kindred Spirits Ascend**

In twilight's glow, our souls unite,
With whispered hopes and dreams in flight,
Together we rise, a beacon bright,
Kindred spirits, hearts alight.

Through valleys low and mountains high,
Your voice a song beneath the sky,
In every breath, we learn to fly,
In love's embrace, we're never shy.

The sacred bond that holds us near,
A tapestry of love sincere,
In every laugh, in every tear,
Kindred spirits, without fear.

Through paths unknown, we take the leap,
In faith we trust, in love we keep,
Together, sacred promises deep,
In harmony, our souls will reap.

## The Divine Mosaic

In every heart, a piece divine,
Crafted with care, by hands of Light,
A unique puzzle, bright design,
In the divine mosaic, we unite.

Each shard reflects a story told,
In colors rich, in shadows fair,
Every spirit, a tale of old,
A masterpiece beyond compare.

Through love we gather, side by side,
In joyful unity, we soar,
Embracing life, no need to hide,
In the mosaic, hearts explore.

Each fragment shines, each voice a song,
Through all the storms, we stand as one,
In harmony, where we belong,
Together woven, 'til we're done.

## The Guiding Star of Belonging

In the night sky shines a light,
A beacon for hearts in flight.
With each glimmer, hope ignites,
Drawing souls to sacred heights.

In unity, we find our place,
In every smile, a warm embrace.
Together, we rise and sing,
As one, in love, we take wing.

Through trials faced, we stand strong,
In faith, we know we belong.
With each step, we tread the path,
Guided by love's holy wrath.

Under the watch of sacred stars,
We overcome all earthly scars.
In harmony, our spirits soar,
Connected now, forevermore.

Let the world hear our call,
In togetherness, we are all.
Through shadows, our spirits gleam,
In belonging, we form a team.

**A Testament of Togetherness**

In the hands of the faithful, we stand,
Bound by love, a sacred band.
Our voices rise, a melody bright,
In harmony, we seek the light.

With every prayer, a seed is sown,
In soil of hope, we've brightly grown.
Together, we weather the storm,
In the refuge of love, we are warm.

Blessed by the ties of soul to soul,
In every heart, we find our role.
As rivers flow and mountains rise,
In unity, our spirits surprise.

Echoes of faith, aloft in the air,
Remind us all we're meant to share.
As branches stretch towards the sky,
In loving arms, we're destined to fly.

Let this testament be our guide,
In togetherness, we shall abide.
Through every trial that life may send,
In each other, we shall depend.

## Embracing the Eternal Essence

In the stillness of the dawn,
We hear a whisper, love reborn.
With open hearts, we dare to see,
The essence of eternity.

Each moment shared, a sacred gift,
In every touch, our spirits lift.
We dance in joy, we weep in grace,
Embracing every soul's embrace.

Through the trials, we journey on,
Together, never truly alone.
With every heartbeat, love aligns,
Eternal essence in our designs.

In the tapestry of life, we weave,
Threads of hope, we shall believe.
Through valleys low and mountains high,
In unity, our spirits fly.

Let the dawn break with sacred light,
Illuminating dark with bright.
In every moment, may we find,
The eternal essence intertwined.

## A Light upon the Pilgrim's Path

In shadows deep, we seek the flame,
A guiding light, so pure, so tame.
With faith to lead, we journey forth,
Upon this road, we find our worth.

The winding way, with trials rife,
Yet every step sings of new life.
Hand in hand, we feel the grace,
A warm embrace, a sacred place.

The stars above, they watch and gleam,
Echoing our hopes and dreams.
Through darkest night, our spirits soar,
With every heartbeat, we implore.

So let us walk, with hearts aligned,
In love and peace, our souls entwined.
Together strong, we rise and stand,
In light we trust, guided by His hand.

A light remains, unwavering, bright,
For every pilgrim lost in night.
Boundless grace, forever here,
Through every doubt, we persevere.

## Heartfelt Homilies in Motion

Words that drift like gentle rain,
Nourishing hearts, easing the pain.
In every tale, a truth unfolds,
With love's embrace, our spirit holds.

In quiet murmurs, wisdom speaks,
Through humble hearts, our spirit seeks.
Every lesson, a sacred thread,
Weaving paths where angels tread.

Time marches on, yet we remain,
In every joy, in every gain.
The echoes of our voices rise,
A symphony beneath the skies.

With every step, we share the light,
Transforming darkness into sight.
Through trials faced, we grow in grace,
Finding solace in His embrace.

Heartfelt homilies, pure and true,
Bonding each with sacred view.
Together we dance, in faith's embrace,
Guided by love, our saving grace.

## Convergence of the Devout

From distant shores, we hear the call,
To gather round, to stand up tall.
In unity, our voices rise,
A chorus blessed beneath the skies.

With faith as anchor, hearts in tune,
We draw together, morning to noon.
In every prayer, a promise made,
Through love's forever, never to fade.

In gentle whispers, we find our way,
In fellowship, we choose to stay.
Each spirit shines, a beacon bright,
Guiding lost souls through the night.

Our bodies join, but souls align,
In sacred dance, divine design.
As rivers flow to meet the sea,
So too, we find our unity.

In convergence grand, we find our peace,
A tapestry of love's increase.
Together strong, we walk this path,
In faith and trust, we find our hearth.

## The Kindred Call of the Universe

Stars that twinkle, spirits greet,
Kindred souls in cosmic beat.
Together we rise, on winds of grace,
In the vastness, we find our place.

Galaxies weave a sacred song,
In harmony, we all belong.
With open hearts, we heed the sound,
In every whisper, love is found.

The universe hums a gentle tune,
Reflecting light of sun and moon.
We dance beneath, in sacred time,
Connecting all, in faith's sweet rhyme.

Through every shadow, through every light,
We journey forth, embracing night.
Bound by threads that never break,
In love's embrace, our souls awake.

A kindred call that fills the air,
Uniting hearts, a sacred prayer.
In cosmic dance, we twirl and spin,
Forever intertwined, we begin.

## **Bound by Spiritual Threads**

In shadows deep, we find our light,
A whisper soft, guiding our night.
Threads unseen, weaves in the soul,
Together we rise, together we whole.

With prayers like wings, we soar above,
Connected in spirit, bound by love.
Each heart a note in the hymn divine,
Singing of faith, as stars align.

Through trials faced, our strength we claim,
In faith's embrace, we speak His name.
A tapestry rich, in colors bright,
Woven together, through darkness and light.

In silence shared, our souls converse,
With sacred texts, we gently immerse.
Threads of belief bind us in grace,
A sacred circle, a holy space.

Together we stand, hands raised in prayer,
In unbroken bonds, our souls laid bare.
For in this union, we truly see,
The divine's reflection, in you and me.

## Reflections of the Infinite

In every heart lies a mirrored truth,
A spark of the divine, a thread of youth.
The infinite whispers in each passing breeze,
A testament written in the trees.

Look to the stars where silence reigns,
Where eternity dances, unbroken chains.
In moments and memories, spirit shall flow,
The essence of love in the ebb and the glow.

With every heartbeat, a song is sung,
An echo of ages, where hope is sprung.
Reflections of light in the shadows we chase,
In the depths of despair, we find His grace.

Through valleys deep and mountains high,
We seek the eternal, we long to fly.
In the gentle dawn, our voices blend,
With trust in the heavens, our spirits mend.

As waves of the ocean return to the shore,
In cycles of life, we are evermore.
In unity, we find our sacred part,
Reflections of love, within every heart.

## Murmurs of the Believers

In the stillness, hear the soft refrain,
Murmurs of believers, joy mixed with pain.
Whispers of hope, in shadows unite,
Guiding each other through the long night.

With hands held high, we share our fears,
Pouring our hearts, mingling our tears.
The echoes of faith, like raindrops fall,
In the garden of love, we answer His call.

Each story a thread in the fabric of life,
Through moments of peace, through sorrow and strife.
In sacred circles, we gather and pray,
Murmurs of trust, lighting the way.

With soft-spoken words, we lift each soul,
Creating a bond, making us whole.
For in every whisper, a promise lies,
Murmurs of truth, reaching the skies.

From dawn's early light, till the night's last breath,
In unity's warmth, we conquer death.
Murmurs of believers, our spirits set free,
In the chorus of life, we find harmony.

## The Fold of the Faithful

In the fold of the faithful, we gather near,
To share our burdens, to dry each tear.
With open hearts, our voices blend,
In love's embrace, we seek to mend.

Through laughter and sorrow, in joy we share,
Hand in hand, we breathe the prayer.
The warmth of the spirit surrounds our space,
In the fold of the faithful, we find His grace.

In the stories told, the lessons learned,
The flame of belief forever burned.
Each soul a candle, flickering bright,
In unity's glow, we chase the night.

With gentle whispers, we offer our peace,
In forgiveness found, our hearts release.
For in every trial, together we stand,
In the fold of the faithful, we live hand in hand.

As seasons change and time like rivers flows,
In the embrace of faith, connection grows.
In the fold of the faithful, love holds sway,
A sanctuary bright as the dawn of day.

# The Holy Hearth of Kindred Spirits

In the glow of sacred flame,
Where souls unite, and love's the name,
Hands entwined in prayer we stand,
Kindred spirits, heart to hand.

A bond unbroken, pure and bright,
Under stars that pierce the night,
Whispered hopes and dreams we share,
In this warmth, we feel the care.

Through trials faced, we grow in grace,
Bound by faith in this holy place,
Each moment cherished, none forget,
In kindred hearts, no room for regret.

When shadows cast their fleeting doubt,
Together strong, we turn about,
For in this hearth, our spirits soar,
Love ignites and opens doors.

Together walking life's long road,
With every step, our hearts bestowed,
In the light of truth, we find our way,
Guided by love, come what may.

## Cradled by Celestial Grace

In the morning dew, we rise anew,
Surrounded by love, ever true,
Heaven's blessing falls like rain,
Cradled in grace, released from pain.

With whispers soft, the angels sing,
To hearts that seek the hope they bring,
Each note a promise, pure delight,
Guiding us through the darkest night.

In every trial, we find a sign,
A tender touch, a love divine,
Through valleys low and mountains high,
With faith in heart, we learn to fly.

The stars above, they light our way,
Reminding us to pause and pray,
For in the silence, truth is found,
In celestial love, our souls abound.

Together we'll journey, hand in hand,
In the embrace of love so grand,
With every heartbeat, we draw near,
Cradled by grace, we'll cast off fear.

## In the Embrace of Faith

Through tempest winds, we find our peace,
In faith's embrace, we seek release,
With open hearts, we share our plight,
Together walking toward the light.

Each gentle prayer a whispered sigh,
In love's warm grasp, fears pass us by,
A tapestry of lives entwined,
In the embrace of faith, we find.

With steadfast hearts, we'll forge ahead,
On paths of hope where angels tread,
For every challenge, every fall,
In faith's embrace, we stand tall.

Through trials faced, we learn to bend,
In every heart, a steadfast friend,
Faith lights the way through darkest days,
In the embrace of love, we praise.

Together we rise, in unity strong,
Finding solace in each song,
In the embrace of faith so wide,
With love as guide, we will abide.

## Unveiling the Divine Interval

In moments still, we seek the source,
A sacred pause, a gentle force,
In the silence, whispers clear,
Unveiling truth, drawing near.

Each heartbeat sings, a hymn of grace,
In the divine, we find our place,
Where time dissolves, and souls ignite,
In love's embrace, we take our flight.

When shadows loom, and doubts arise,
We close our eyes and see the skies,
For in the interval of time,
The sacred dance, a love sublime.

As sunlight breaks through morning mist,
In every moment, we persist,
For in each breath, the spirit flows,
Unveiling love as wisdom grows.

In fellowship, we greet the day,
With open hearts, we find the way,
Through every interval, deep and wide,
We walk together, side by side.

# The Pilgrimage of the Heart

In quiet morn, the heart takes flight,
Through valleys deep, in sacred light.
With faith as guide, the soul does tread,
On paths where ancient blessings spread.

Each step a prayer, a whispered sigh,
In shadows soft, we reach for high.
Mountains rise, yet spirits soar,
In love's embrace, we seek for more.

The journey long, with burdens shared,
In unity, our hearts are bared.
With every ache, a lesson learned,
In pilgrimage, our souls are turned.

The road unfolds, where angels sing,
With open hands, we gift the King.
In laughter bright and tears of grace,
We find our strength, our holy place.

With every star that lights the night,
We gather hope, we gather might.
In faith, we rise, as one, we stand,
In pilgrimage, we walk hand in hand.

## Dwelling in Divine Presence

In stillness found, the heart does rest,
In sacred space, we seek the blessed.
With every breath, a soft embrace,
In quietude, we find His grace.

The world may spin, but here we stay,
In love's pure light, we find our way.
With open eyes, we see the glow,
In divine presence, hearts do flow.

The whispers soft, like gentle rain,
In every joy, in every pain.
With gratitude, our spirits rise,
In His embrace, the soul replies.

The sacred sound, a hymn of praise,
A melody that guides our days.
In harmony, we find our song,
In dwelling here, we all belong.

In every moment, holy light,
In darkness deep, we feel the bright.
With faith aglow, we journey on,
In divine presence, we are drawn.

## In Search of Sacred Ground

Upon the earth, with weary feet,
We walk the path where shadows meet.
With hopeful hearts, we seek the true,
In search of grace, in search of you.

The mountains call, their peaks so high,
In silent prayer, we lift our cry.
Through forests deep, where spirits dwell,
In whispers soft, we hear His bell.

Each step we take, a quest begun,
In every heart, His love is spun.
With open hands, we reach for light,
In sacred ground, we find our sight.

We wander through the sacred stones,
In every breeze, His presence roams.
With every prayer, a truth we find,
In search of ground, our souls aligned.

In unity, we stand as one,
With faith that melts the morning sun.
Each sacred breath, a gift profound,
In search of peace, we find the sound.

## The Refuge of the Righteous

In times of strife, a shelter shines,
The refuge found in sacred signs.
With arms outstretched, we gather close,
In love's embrace, we find our host.

The righteous walk on paths of light,
With every heart, they spark the night.
In unity, their voices blend,
With every prayer, our spirits mend.

Through trials faced, we stand as one,
In faith reborn, we greet the sun.
With wisdom deep, our hearts aligned,
In refuge strong, our souls refined.

When shadows fall, we lift our gaze,
In every moment, He is praised.
The refuge holds, our spirits soar,
In righteous love, we seek for more.

In quiet night, when stars are bright,
We dwell in peace, in holy light.
With gratitude, our hearts obey,
In refuge found, we choose His way.

**The Light of Many Lanterns**

In the stillness of the night,
Guided by the stars so bright,
Lanterns flicker, softly glow,
Carrying love where'er we go.

Each flame a prayer, each light a hope,
Uniting hearts, helping us cope,
In the darkness, we find a way,
Together we stand, come what may.

Wisdom whispers in the breeze,
In every moment, our souls find peace,
With every lantern, the shadows fade,
The promise of dawn, our spirits invade.

As the night turns into day,
The lanterns guide our earnest way,
Blessed by the light, we journey on,
In the heart of grace, our fears are gone.

So let us gather, side by side,
With the light of faith as our guide,
Through every trial, we will discern,
The love that waits, the light we yearn.

## Cradle of My Soul

In the quiet of the evening light,
I seek the solace of Your might,
Cradled safe in love's embrace,
In this stillness, I find grace.

Through the shadows, I will roam,
Knowing, Lord, You are my home,
Whispers of peace in every sound,
In Your arms, my hopes abound.

With every breath, Your presence near,
In trials faced, I have no fear,
The cradle of my soul so pure,
In You, my heart finds hope sure.

Each moment spent, an endless prayer,
In longing times, I feel You there,
The gentle tide of love unfurls,
Embracing me, transforming worlds.

So let my spirit rise and sing,
With gratitude, my heart will cling,
To the sacred haven where I dwell,
In the cradle of love, all is well.

## **The Divine Hearth**

At the hearth of truth, flames dance bright,
Warmth of spirit, casting light,
Gathered close, our hearts entwine,
In the love that feels divine.

The crackling fire sings a song,
Reminding us where we belong,
In the rays of grace, shadows retreat,
In this haven, our souls meet.

Beneath the stars, the night is still,
With open hearts, we find His will,
In every ember, the promise glows,
The path of love forever shows.

Through every trial, storms may break,
The hearth remains when all else shakes,
In the sacred warmth, fears take flight,
Together, we rise, in faith's pure light.

So come and sit, let worries cease,
In this dwelling, find your peace,
At the Divine Hearth, love ignites,
Guiding us through the darkest nights.

## A Journey to Sacred Ground

With each step, I seek the place,
Where grace gathers, time gives chase,
On sacred ground, my spirit soars,
In the quiet, my heart restores.

Through valleys low and mountains high,
The whispers of love always nigh,
In the faces of the kind,
I glimpse the light that guides the blind.

Every soul a story told,
With dreams and hopes, in faith, we hold,
As we wander, our burdens shared,
In unity, the heart is bared.

The sacred ground beneath our feet,
Echoes with love, profound and sweet,
Through trials faced, we find our way,
With every step, we learn to pray.

So let us walk this path unknown,
Together, never left alone,
On a journey where love abounds,
We shall rise on sacred grounds.

## **Guiding Light in the Wilderness**

In shadows deep, where doubts abide,
A beacon shines, our hearts to guide.
Through barren lands, we walk in trust,
With faith as firm, as sacred dust.

The stars align, a heavenly call,
In silence heard, we rise, not fall.
With every step, the path is clear,
Our souls entwined, the Lord draws near.

Each twisted route, a lesson learned,
In every trial, our spirits burned.
The tempest strong, yet we stand fast,
For love divine, our anchor cast.

So take my hand, and fear no more,
Together drawn, to heaven's shore.
In wilderness, we find the light,
A guiding star, through darkest night.

## Among the Faithful

In humble prayer, we gather round,
In every heart, His love is found.
Voices rise, a sacred hymn,
In joyful praise, our spirits swim.

In trials shared, we find our strength,
Together walk, in love's pure length.
With open arms, we comfort so,
In unity, our spirits grow.

The bonds we build, they cannot break,
In every smile, His grace we take.
Among the faithful, we unite,
A tapestry of purest light.

So let us stand, through storm and fire,
In service true, and hearts' desire.
For in this place, His presence stays,
Among the faithful, we lift praise.

## The Spirit's Homecoming

From distant shores, the spirit flies,
To find its rest, beneath the skies.
In whispered winds, a gentle call,
To find the peace, that conquers all.

With open hearts, we seek the way,
In softest light, our fears decay.
As blossoms bloom, in sacred grace,
Our souls embrace, a warm embrace.

No longer lost, we find our place,
In every tear, a trace of grace.
The past dissolves, in love's pure stream,
Awakened now, to hope's sweet dream.

So rise anew, with every breath,
In joy we find, the dance of death.
The spirit's flight, a wondrous song,
In unity, we all belong.

## A Pathway to Eden

In garden vast, the promise waits,
A pathway clear, the heart creates.
With every step, in faith we tread,
Through fragrant blooms, our spirits fed.

The morning light, a tender kiss,
In harmony, we find our bliss.
With open eyes, we seek His face,
In every moment, feel His grace.

From every thorn, a flower grows,
In trials faced, our wisdom shows.
With hands in prayer, our hearts align,
A pathway true, where love does shine.

Through every trial, through every tear,
The promise stands, forever near.
In Eden's glow, we'll find our way,
In love's embrace, we choose to stay.

## Embracing My Sacred Roots

In the whispering winds, I find my song,
Binding threads of old, where I belong.
With each gentle prayer, my spirit soars,
Embracing the love from ancient shores.

The earth beneath me holds the tale,
Of ancestors' strength that will not fail.
With every heartbeat, I feel them near,
Guiding my path, dispelling fear.

In the dance of twilight, I bow my head,
To the wisdom of the past, where I'm led.
Roots intertwined in sacred ground,
In unity with creation, I am found.

Awakened by light that streams from above,
I walk in harmony, filled with love.
My sacred roots keep me so aligned,
In the garden of faith, my soul defined.

## The Hallowed Hall of Unity

In the hallowed hall, voices rise,
Sing of peace beneath the skies.
Together we stand, hands intertwined,
In the warmth of love, all hearts aligned.

The echoes of hope, a soothing balm,
In the embrace of faith, we find calm.
Where divisions fade, harmony blooms,
In unity's song, every spirit looms.

With candles lit, we share our light,
Guiding each other through the night.
In a tapestry woven by grace,
We find our purpose, our rightful place.

Let us gather, both great and small,
In the sacred space, within the call.
The hallowed hall sings, a heavenly tune,
As we journey on, beneath the moon.

## Reaching for Redemption

With open hands, I reach for grace,
In humble prayer, I find my place.
The weight of sin, I lay aside,
In the redeeming love, I will abide.

Each step I take, the path is clear,
Guided by faith, I cast my fear.
The past may haunt, but I rise anew,
In the light of mercy, my heart breaks through.

The chains that bind, now fall away,
In the arms of truth, I'm here to stay.
With every tear, a lesson learned,
In the face of love, my spirit burned.

Reaching for redemption, I find my voice,
In the journey of healing, I rejoice.
By grace, I'll soar, my spirit free,
Embracing the truth of who I'm meant to be.

## Sanctuary in the Silence

In the hush of dawn, my heart prepares,
A sanctuary found in silence rare.
Away from the noise, my spirit retreats,
In stillness, a map where presence meets.

The whispers of the soul, a gentle guide,
In the quietude, I will abide.
With every breath, peace floods my mind,
A sacred space for love, I find.

Here, in the silence, the world fades away,
In soft reverie, I choose to stay.
And in this moment, clarity sings,
In sanctuary, I'm crowned with wings.

Allowing the light to shine within,
In the embrace of silence, I begin.
My heart a vessel, ever so wide,
In the stillness, I am not denied.

## Beyond the Veil of Solitude

In silence deep the whispers reach,
A call from realms where spirits teach.
The heart ascends from earthly bind,
Beyond the veil, true peace we find.

The nightingale sings in the hush of night,
A feathered prayer takes wing in flight.
In solitude, the soul draws near,
To find within, the love sincere.

With every tear, a seed is sown,
In barren lands, new life is grown.
In quietude, our voices blend,
Eternal truths that never end.

The stars above, they sing in rhyme,
Connecting hearts across the time.
Through solitude, we come to see,
The sacred thread that binds you and me.

Beneath the stars, we stand as one,
Embracing shadows, fears undone.
In the stillness, knowledge flows,
Beyond the veil, where spirit glows.

## Stones of the Ancients

In the quiet earth beneath our feet,
Lie stories buried, wise and sweet.
Stones of the ancients, silent they stand,
Guarding secrets of this holy land.

Each grain of sand, a tale untold,
Of prayers whispered, of faith bold.
In the shadows of the mountains high,
We seek the truth that will not die.

The rivers run deep, their waters pure,
A hymn of ages, we must endure.
In nature's cradle, we find our place,
As we walk in the stones of grace.

With every echo of thunder's roll,
The past reminds us to reclaim our soul.
Ancient wisdom, like whispers, flow,
Binding the present to what we know.

As we gather round the sacred fire,
We lift our hearts in praise and choir.
For in these stones, the spirit thrives,
Embracing all that truly lives.

## In the Fold of Grace

In the fold of grace, we softly dwell,
Wrapped in love, the heart's sweet spell.
A gentle touch, a kind embrace,
Uniting souls in sacred space.

The breath of dawn ignites our hopes,
Through trials faced, the spirit copes.
In moments still, we find our way,
Guided by light, the breaking day.

Each step we take, a sacred vow,
In love's embrace, we learn to bow.
Together as one, we rise and fall,
In the fold of grace, we hear the call.

The whispers of angels part the air,
Reminding us that we all share.
In every heartbeat, a melody plays,
Holding us close in love's sweet gaze.

Through trials and triumphs, we endure,
In the fold of grace, we find what's pure.
Transcending time, our spirits roam,
In unity, we find our home.

# Fabrics of Connection

In the fabrics of connection, threads entwined,
Woven by hands of the divine.
Each life a pattern, a story spun,
Together we shine, united as one.

Across the mountains, over the sea,
The threads of love bind you and me.
In every heartbeat, a tapestry grows,
Color and texture, the spirit glows.

From woven fibers, we draw our strength,
In the depths of silence, we find our length.
The whispers of time echo through space,
In the fabrics of connection, we find our grace.

The hands that gather, the hearts that mend,
Through joy and sorrow, we shall transcend.
In every stitch, a lesson learned,
In love's vast quilt, our souls are turned.

Together we grow, together we thrive,
In the fabrics of connection, we come alive.
As we journey forth, hand in hand,
We weave a future, a sacred land.

## **Altar of Belonging**

In shadows deep, we gather near,
With humble hearts, we shed our fear.
Each whispered prayer, a sacred thread,
In unity, our spirits led.

The flame of hope, a guiding light,
In darkest times, it holds us tight.
Together as one, we find our place,
In this embrace, we seek His grace.

Through trials faced, we stand so strong,
In faith we find where we belong.
Each blessing shared, a sacred bond,
Our voices lift, a joyful song.

With every tear, a river flows,
In love we heal, the heart's repose.
The altar built on trust and care,
In every soul, His presence there.

So let us serve with hearts so true,
In every deed, His light shines through.
Together bound, forever free,
Upon this altar, we shall be.

## Roots in Celestial Soil

From ancient skies, the blessings pour,
In fertile hearts, our spirits soar.
With roots that spread in heavenly ground,
In unity, our hopes are found.

Beneath the stars, we find our stake,
With every breath, a promise we make.
The whispers of the wise proclaim,
In sacred soil, we find our name.

Through trials faced, we bend, not break,
In every choice, the path we take.
A garden rich with love and grace,
In faith, we find our rightful place.

The branches reach toward the divine,
In every heart, a sacred shrine.
With fruits of kindness, hope, and peace,
In giving, we find sweet release.

So let us grow, entwined as one,
In every dawn, behold the sun.
With roots in soil that never fades,
We walk with Him through all cascades.

## **Tapestry of Faith**

Weaving threads of hope and grace,
In every heart, a sacred place.
With colors bright, our stories blend,
In faith, we find our journey's end.

Each stitch a prayer, each knot a bond,
Together strong, we journey on.
The tapestry of life unfolds,
In His embrace, our truth it holds.

Through trials faced, we seek the light,
In darkest days, we stand upright.
With woven hearts and open hands,
We share our dreams, our love expands.

In every tear, a thread of gold,
A tale of hope is gently told.
With every joy and sorrow shared,
In this design, we are prepared.

So let us stitch with hearts aglow,
In unity, our spirits grow.
This tapestry of faith we weave,
In love's embrace, we shall believe.

## Haven of the Wanderer

In journeys long, we seek a shore,
A haven safe, forevermore.
With weary feet, we hymn our song,
In love's embrace, we all belong.

The mountains high, the valleys low,
Each path we tread, His love will show.
With open hearts, we find our way,
In every dawn, a brand new day.

Through storms and trials, we hold fast,
In every moment, kindness cast.
The shelter found in love's warm gaze,
In weary nights, His mercy stays.

With fellow souls, our stories blend,
Each gentle hand, a faithful friend.
In this haven, we give and share,
In every breath, His presence there.

So let us wander, hand in hand,
In sacred spaces, forever stand.
This haven built on trust and grace,
In every heart, a holy place.

## A Homeward Pilgrimage

In fields of grace, we walk in light,
With every step, our hearts unite.
A path of faith, so true, we tread,
In search of peace, where hope is fed.

Through valleys deep and mountains high,
We lift our eyes towards the sky.
Each prayer a whisper, soft and clear,
A call to love, to draw us near.

With shadows cast by doubts and fears,
We stand together, dry our tears.
The holy hymn, it guides our way,
A song of grace, for night and day.

In every heart, a spark divine,
Through trials faced, our souls align.
The road may twist, the journey long,
But in our faith, we grow more strong.

So onward, pilgrims, hand in hand,
By sacred realms, we'll learn to stand.
Our homeward quest will never cease,
In love's embrace, we find our peace.

## The Light that Guides Us

In darkest nights, a beacon bright,
It pierces through with holy light.
A gentle glow, a steady flame,
That whispers softly, calls our name.

Through stormy seas and trials sore,
We seek the path, forevermore.
With courage bound, we rise anew,
The guiding light will see us through.

From ancient texts, the wisdom flows,
In every word, the Spirit glows.
We walk with grace in every stride,
In faith, our souls shall abide.

In shadows deep, we find our way,
The light of love shall break the day.
A sacred spark, it leads us home,
In every heart, we are not alone.

So let us shine, let voices sing,
With every breath, our praises ring.
The light that guides will never fade,
In grace and truth, our hopes are made.

## **Heaven's Embrace**

Above the clouds, where angels dwell,
A love profound, we know so well.
With open arms, they greet the soul,
In heaven's grace, we are made whole.

Through trials faced on earthly ground,
In whispered prayers, our peace is found.
The promise made, through love divine,
In heaven's arms, our spirits shine.

As lilies bloom and rivers flow,
The heart finds peace amidst the woe.
With every breath, we rise and soar,
In heaven's embrace, forevermore.

The journey's end, where joys await,
Entwined in love, we celebrate.
From earthly cares, our souls release,
In heaven's arms, we find our peace.

So let us seek, with hearts so true,
The love that binds both me and you.
In every moment, let us see,
The heaven's grace that sets us free.

## The Sanctuary of the Soul

In quiet hearts, a sacred space,
Where whispers dwell of God's embrace.
A sanctuary, pure and bright,
That shines with hope through darkest night.

With every breath, we seek to find,
The peace bestowed on heart and mind.
In prayer and silence, love unfolds,
A story deep that must be told.

Through trials faced and burdens borne,
In faith's warm light, we find reborn.
The soul's true shelter, ever near,
In sanctuary, there's no fear.

With kindred spirits at our side,
In unity, we turn the tide.
Each step we take, a dance of grace,
In the sanctuary, we find our place.

So lift your eyes, embrace the day,
In love's vast arms, let worries sway.
For in the heart, the truth is whole,
The sanctuary of the soul.

## In Search of the Sacred Flame

In the stillness of the dawn's embrace,
I seek the fire that lights my grace.
With hands uplifted, heart exposed,
I wander forth where faith is closed.

Through valleys deep and mountains high,
The sacred flame is nigh, I cry.
For every shadow cast by doubt,
A flickering light can pull me out.

With every prayer, a step I take,
In search of wisdom, truths awake.
The embers of hope burn ever bright,
Guiding me through the endless night.

As whispers linger in the air,
I clutch the flame with tender care.
In unity with the divine glow,
My spirit soars, my heart will know.

So here I stand with fervent soul,
In reverence, I find my whole.
For in the search, I uncover fate,
The sacred flame will not abate.

## The Garden of the Graced

In the garden where the faithful tread,
Soft petals bloom where angels led.
Each fragrant whisper tells a tale,
Of grace abound beyond the pale.

Beneath the branches, shade bestows,
A sacred hush where spirit grows.
With every leaf that drapes the ground,
The love of heaven can be found.

In colors bright and shadows long,
The heart is lifted, pure and strong.
With every step, a prayer's seed,
In this hallowed place, my soul is freed.

The fruits of labor bless the earth,
In gratitude, I find my worth.
In every sunrise, hope's refrain,
The garden sings of joy and pain.

So come and wander, find your grace,
In this sacred, loving space.
With humble heart, and faith embraced,
In the garden, we are graced.

# The Path of the Devout

Along the path where many roam,
The weary wander, seeking home.
With footfalls light, and spirit high,
They journey forth beneath the sky.

The stones are worn by time and tears,
Each step unveils the path of years.
With every breath, the heart aligns,
To sacred truths and whispered signs.

Through trials faced and burdens borne,
The faithful rise with light reborn.
In every heart, the echo rings,
That love and hope are precious things.

In valleys low and peaks of grace,
The path unfolds in endless space.
With every choice, the soul finds light,
In devotion's glow, we take flight.

So walk with me, dear soul aligned,
In faith, we find what's pure and kind.
Through every step, let love be sought,
On the path of the devout, we've fought.

## Whispers from the Soul's Abyss

In the depths where shadows creep,
The soul sings softly, secrets keep.
Amidst the dark, a gentle light,
Calls forth the dawn, dispels the night.

A hollow echo of past despair,
Yet whispers rise in stillness there.
The heart, though weary, beats anew,
With faith as anchor, pure and true.

In struggles faced, where pain does dwell,
The soul's abyss can weave a spell.
Yet even in the darkest place,
A spark ignites through love's embrace.

So listen close to whispers fine,
For in the depths, the spirit shines.
In every trial, a lesson learned,
In ashes, see how fervor burned.

From depths of sorrow, hope will rise,
To greet the dawn with open skies.
So let the whispers guide you forth,
From the soul's abyss, embrace your worth.

## The Gathering of Souls

In silence we gather, hearts intertwined,
Voices like whispers, a sacred design.
From shadows we rise, with love as our guide,
In faith we unite, with spirits aligned.

The light gently beckons, our burdens laid bare,
In prayer we are woven, each soul laid to care.
Through trials we journey, hand in hand we stand,
A tapestry woven, by divine, gentle hand.

With hope in our hearts, we seek and we find,
The grace that envelops, our fears left behind.
In moments of sorrow, together we weep,
Yet joy in our laughter, a promise to keep.

As echoes of love in this gathering swell,
The stories of lives, each one weaves a spell.
A circle unbroken, of brotherhood, sister,
In the eyes of the lost, we are all there to witness.

In the gathering twilight, a blessing we share,
The whispers of heaven are felt in the air.
We rise with the dawn, on wings of the night,
In unity's embrace, we walk toward the light.

## Embracing the Uncharted

With courage we venture, where few have tread,
In search of the truth, where the living have led.
Each step is a prayer, each breath a new song,
In the arms of the unknown, we feel we belong.

The stars are our compass, the moon our guide,
In solitude's whispers, our hearts open wide.
We seek what is holy, the path yet unknown,
In silence we gather, we're never alone.

With faith as our lantern, illuminating dark,
We traverse the wilderness, igniting a spark.
For every lost soul, in the shadows that creep,
There lies a true beauty, a promise to keep.

In the depths of our journey, we find what is real,
The strength in connection, the truth we can feel.
As mountains may tremble, and storms may arise,
In love's gentle arms, we discover the skies.

With each newfound valley, we gather the light,
Embracing the uncharted, we bask in the bright.
In the spirit of seeking, our hearts intertwine,
Together we flourish, with hope as our vine.

## The Eternal Family

In the circle of time, we find our embrace,
Connected in spirit, in love, and in grace.
Through ages we flourish, through trials we grow,
In the heart of the family, our light we bestow.

With roots that run deep, like the grandest of trees,
We gather together, a chorus of peace.
Through laughter and sorrow, in all that we share,
The bonds of affection shine bright and lay bare.

Each moment a treasure, each memory a gift,
In the warmth of our circle, our spirits uplift.
As seasons may change, and paths may diverge,
In love everlasting, together we merge.

In every reunion, the echoes resound,
With stories of hope, our shared love profound.
The meaning of family, a tapestry spun,
In the heart of the world, we shine like the sun.

With wisdom from ages, our legacy grows,
In unity's cradle, our true essence shows.
As we walk hand in hand, let our voices proclaim,
In the soul of our family, we'll always remain.

## An Offering to the Lost

We gather in silence, with hearts open wide,
An offering tender, for souls that have cried.
In shadows of longing, where hopes seem to fade,
We send forth our love, as a gentle cascade.

With prayers like petals, we shower the ground,
For the lost and the weary, may solace be found.
In the depths of their sorrow, our voices we raise,
In love's sweetest language, we offer our praise.

Through valleys of anguish, our spirits will roam,
To light up the darkness, to guide them back home.
An offering pure, from the depths of our soul,
In the name of compassion, we strive to console.

From the ashes of sorrow, we kindle the flame,
In the hearts of the lost, call each one by name.
In unity's embrace, let our hearts intertwine,
As we bring forth the hope, a love that can shine.

With each falling tear, a promise is made,
For the lost and the lonely, no longer afraid.
An offering of courage, of faith that remains,
In every lost spirit, a love that sustains.

In the stillness of night, as the stars softly gleam,
We gather as one, in a beautiful dream.
An offering to the lost, in the name of the free,
May they find their own path, and forever be.

## Upon Holy Ground

We gather in reverence, hearts aligned,
The whispers of heaven, softly we find.
With each step we take, we tread so light,
Upon holy ground, bathed in holy light.

In silence we bow, our spirits rise,
We seek the divine, the truth in the skies.
The echoes of angels, a sweet serenade,
Guide us through shadows, never afraid.

In prayerful devotion, we stand as one,
With faith as our shield, we face the sun.
The blessings that flow, like rivers they stream,
Granting us courage, igniting our dream.

The path that we walk, though rugged and steep,
Is lighted by grace, a promise to keep.
Each moment we cherish, each breath is a prize,
Awakening hope, where love never dies.

United in purpose, our mission is clear,
To love and to serve, casting out fear.
Upon holy ground, together we stand,
As children of light, guided by His hand.

## Ancestral Echoes and Ascendant Dreams

In the whispers of past, our roots intertwine,
Ancestral echoes, a sacred sign.
We honor their struggles, their love we embrace,
Carrying forward their strength and grace.

As dreams rise and soar, we reach for the sky,
With visions of hope, our spirits fly high.
The stars are a map, guiding our way,
In the dance of the night, we find our sway.

Each heartbeat a testimony, each breath a prayer,
To the legacy left, we solemnly care.
The fire of courage ignites in our soul,
Uniting our past to the dreams we extol.

With wisdom inherited, we walk the path bright,
Embracing our truth, we step into light.
The future is ours, we reach for the beam,
In the echoes of ancestors, we weave our dream.

So let us ascend on wings of pure love,
With grace as our guide from the heavens above.
Ancestral echoes, our honor, our pride,
In unity strong, together we stride.

## Dwelling in the Light

In the stillness of morning, the dawn softly glows,
Inviting our hearts where the pure river flows.
Dwelling in light, we find peace and grace,
In the warmth of His love, a sacred embrace.

The shadows may linger, but they cannot stay,
For faith is our beacon, and guides our way.
In whispers of mercy, we find sweet release,
A promise fulfilled, we hold onto peace.

With each gentle breeze, we feel His caress,
Dwelling in light brings a heart's tenderness.
The choir of angels, their harmony sings,
Lifting our spirits on glorious wings.

From trials faced boldly, we rise ever strong,
With gratitude flowing, we know we belong.
In the tapestry woven of love and delight,
Together we flourish, dwelling in light.

With faith unshaken, we journey ahead,
In the glow of His wisdom, our spirits are fed.
In the dance of salvation, we twirl and we play,
Dwelling in light, we seek His way.

## The Faithful Pursuit

In the dawn of each day, we set our sights high,
With hearts open wide, we reach for the sky.
The faithful pursuit, a journey we tread,
With steps of devotion, where angels have led.

Through trials and storms, our faith will remain,
For love conquers all, and defined is our gain.
With courage we stand, hand in hand we strive,
In the warmth of His grace, our spirits arrive.

We walk with intention, our purpose divine,
In service of others, our hearts intertwine.
With dreams in our hearts, we forge a new trail,
The faithful pursuit, our love will prevail.

So let every moment, reflect His great light,
Embracing each challenge, in shadows so bright.
United we gather, in harmony's song,
In the faithful pursuit, together we belong.

With hope as our compass, we journey ahead,
In the arms of His promise, we shall not dread.
In each faithful step, our purpose rings true,
Guided by love, we renew and pursue.

## The Hidden Blessings of Togetherness

In the quiet moments, we stand side by side,
Hearts entwined, where love cannot hide.
Through whispered prayers and laughter shared,
We find the grace, knowing we are cared.

Together we rise, through valleys and hills,
In each other's presence, our spirit fulfills.
As shadows may linger, we turn towards light,
In unity's embrace, we conquer the night.

Through trials and tears, we walk hand in hand,
Embracing the journey, a sacredland.
With faith as our anchor, we face the unknown,
Finding hidden blessings in seeds we have sown.

In moments of joy, and when hearts are sore,
We gather as one, seeking evermore.
For in togetherness, our souls find their song,
A melody of love, where we both belong.

So let us remember, as paths intertwine,
In the tapestry woven, our spirits align.
Each step a testament, each breath a prayer,
In the hidden blessings of love that we share.

## Streams of Celestial Harmony

In silent communion, we gather in prayer,
Voices like rivers flowing through the air.
Each note a reflection, each word a grace,
Together we seek the divine's warm embrace.

Like stars that are twinkling in the endless night,
Our spirits entwined in a dance of pure light.
With hearts unburdened, we open the door,
To streams of celestial harmony, evermore.

The echoes of kindness, the whispers of love,
Guide us like angels from realms up above.
In every connection, a glimpse of the whole,
We find our completion, one heart, one soul.

Through trials and laughter, we find our true way,
Holding on tightly, come what may.
In the richness of moments, a truth we embrace,
Through streams of harmony, we find our place.

So let us cherish, this bond we have found,
With each pulse of compassion, our spirits abound.
For in togetherness, we harvest the light,
A symphony echoing through the still night.

## Reaching for the Ether

In the stillness of dawn, we reach for the sky,
Fingers stretched out, as the world passes by.
With dreams as our compass, we venture ahead,
Whispers of wisdom, in silence, are spread.

Through valleys of struggle, we navigate fate,
Touching the ether, believing it's great.
With each step we take, let our hearts be our guide,
In the vastness of love, forever abide.

As stars shine above, lighting paths we will roam,
We seek out the warmth, the light of our home.
In unity's glow, we dare to aspire,
Reaching for the ether, igniting the fire.

Through silence and motion, through joy and through pain,
We gather our strength like the softest of rain.
With faith as our anchor, we rise and we soar,
In the realms of the ether, we find so much more.

So let us hold close, this journey we share,
For in each sacred moment, the divine is laid bare.
In reaching for oneness, our spirits ignite,
In the dance of existence, we become the light.

## Sacred Bonds Forged in Fire

In the furnace of trials, our spirits are cast,
Tempered by lessons learned from the past.
Through flames of adversity, we rise like the sun,
Sacred bonds forged, together as one.

With courage and faith, we step through the pyre,
Embracing the heat, igniting desire.
In moments of darkness, when shadows draw near,
We stand strong as iron, refusing to fear.

Each trial a teacher, each struggle a guide,
In the crucible's heart, our true selves reside.
With passion and purpose, our spirits align,
In the sacred creation, our lives intertwine.

Through laughter and tears, we discover our worth,
A tapestry woven from the love of this earth.
For when we are tested, our hearts grow bold,
In the fires of life, real treasures unfold.

So let us remember, in moments of strife,
That strength is revealed in the journey of life.
In bonds forged in fire, we trust and we know,
Together we flourish, together we grow.

## A Haven Beyond Horizons

In the stillness of the night,
Whispers of the stars ignite,
Every soul in search of peace,
Yearns for love that will not cease.

Where the mountains kiss the sky,
And the rivers gently sigh,
A haven waits for those who seek,
A sanctuary for the weak.

Through the valleys, shadows roam,
Yet within, a light calls home,
Hands uplifted, hearts so pure,
In faith's embrace, we find our cure.

Every journey bears a cost,
Yet in love, we are not lost,
With each step, we draw so near,
To the haven we hold dear.

Let our voices rise in song,
In this place, we all belong,
Grace abounds in every prayer,
A haven found beyond all care.

## The Calling of the Believer

In the quiet of the soul,
A gentle whisper calls us whole,
Through the darkness, through the night,
Faith unfurls, a guiding light.

With each heartbeat, echoes clear,
The sacred path we hold so dear,
A call to serve, to love, to be,
By His grace, we shall be free.

When the world seems cold and vast,
We remember those who've passed,
In their footsteps, we will tread,
Following where the Spirit led.

Hands held high, we lift our voice,
In the silence, we rejoice,
Bound by love, we stand as one,
In this calling, we have won.

Oh, believer, come and see,
The beauty of our unity,
In every trial, in every test,
In our faith, we find our rest.

## **Altar of Acceptance**

At the altar, hearts unfold,
Stories shared, both meek and bold,
In acceptance, we find grace,
In every tear, love's embrace.

Here we gather, free from fear,
Casting doubts throughout the year,
Hands entwined, we seek to learn,
From the fire of love we burn.

Every soul a sacred gift,
In our hearts, spirits uplift,
Differences fade in His sight,
Together, we shine so bright.

In acceptance, walls we break,
Through compassion, we awake,
To the joy of kindred souls,
In His light, we are made whole.

Let our hearts be open wide,
To embrace all who confide,
In the love that knows no end,
At the altar, we transcend.

## The Harmony of Heavenly Choirs

In the heavens, soft and sweet,
Voices blend, a rhythmic beat,
Cherubs sing in vibrant tones,
Echoes of eternal homes.

Through the clouds, a chorus flows,
Bringing peace that softly glows,
In the stillness, harmony,
A glimpse of our divinity.

Every note a prayer of love,
Rising high to skies above,
Together as the spirits soar,
Resounding evermore.

In the symphony of light,
Hope emerges, bold and bright,
With each voice, we find our place,
In the warmth of His embrace.

Let us join, both great and small,
In the song that binds us all,
With the angels, we will sing,
In the harmony He brings.

## The Pilgrim's Prayer

O Lord, guide my weary feet,
In paths of light, make my heart beat.
Through valleys low, and mountains tall,
In each humble breath, I hear Your call.

With hands uplifted, I seek Your grace,
In every trial, I find my place.
Oh, grant me strength to bear the load,
In faith I walk, upon Your road.

Through storms of doubt, I hold on tight,
With steadfast hope, I seek the light.
Your mercy flows, a gentle stream,
In whispered prayers, I dare to dream.

As stars above in darkness shine,
I find Your love, so pure, divine.
In every moment, You are near,
My soul's companion, ever clear.

Upon this journey, I lift my eyes,
To promise made beyond the skies.
With every step, I trust in You,
My heart, my guide, forever true.

## **Ascent to the Sacred**

I climb the heights, where shadows flee,
Each step a prayer, my soul to Thee.
With every breath, I feel You near,
In silent awe, I shed my fear.

Upon this path, the spirit rises,
In sacred hills, where truth surprises.
The winds of hope through pine trees sing,
As I ascend, Your love takes wing.

The dawn awakens, a golden hue,
Illuminates the heart that's true.
In every challenge, strength I find,
Guided by wisdom, pure and kind.

With eyes uplifted, I see the vast,
A glimpse of glory, shadows past.
In every moment, I praise Your name,
The sacred fire, an eternal flame.

Upon these heights, I stand renewed,
In humble awe, my spirit viewed.
For in the climb, I come alive,
Embraced by grace, my heart will thrive.

## The Voice of the Divine Whisper

In quiet moments, I hear the call,
A gentle whisper that breaks the fall.
In stillness deep, Your presence glows,
Teaching my heart where compassion flows.

Through trials fierce, Your voice remains,
In darkest hours, You ease my strains.
With love unbound, I feel Your grace,
A soft reminder, I am embraced.

You speak through nature, the rustling leaves,
In every sigh, Your spirit weaves.
A breath of peace, a soothing balm,
In chaotic times, You make me calm.

When doubts surround, and fears arise,
I find my solace in heaven's skies.
Your words of hope, a guiding thread,
In whispers sweet, my spirit's fed.

With every heartbeat, I draw You near,
A sacred bond, forever clear.
For in the silence, I learn to hear,
The voice of love that conquers fear.

## **Nestled in Quietude**

In tranquil fields, where shadows play,
I find a sanctuary, soft as clay.
With every breath, a prayer unfolds,
Nestled in quietude, the heart holds.

The gentle breeze whispers secrets sweet,
In nature's arms, my soul finds peace.
With every rustle and every sigh,
I feel Your presence, ever nigh.

Each flower blooms, a testament true,
Of Your creation, forever new.
In humble moments, grace shines bright,
A soft embrace in the fading light.

Amidst the stillness, my spirit thrives,
In sacred silence, the heart derives.
With open hands, I let love flow,
In peaceful waters, I learn to grow.

For in this space, my burdens cease,
In quietude, I find my peace.
With every heartbeat, I sing Your praise,
Nestled in love, for all my days.

**In Communion with the Divine**

In silence we gather, hearts intertwined,
The whispers of angels, a presence so kind.
In the stillness of night, the truth is revealed,
In sacred communion, our souls are healed.

We lift up our voices, a sweet, gentle song,
To the God who embraces, to whom we belong.
With faith as our anchor, we sail through the storms,
In the light of His love, our spirit transforms.

Through valleys of shadow, His hand is our guide,
In the depth of our trials, He walks by our side.
In prayer, we find power, in worship, we soar,
In communion divine, our hearts yearn for more.

As candles are lit, in the glow we reflect,
On the blessings bestowed, every moment perfect.
Each dawn brings a promise, a chance to renew,
In the warmth of His grace, we rise and break through.

Together we stand, in love's perfect grace,
Hand in hand on this journey, we find our true place.
With peace in our hearts, we spread joy all around,
In communion with the Divine, hope is found.

# The Tapestry of Grace

In every thread woven, a story unfolds,
A tapestry rich, with hues of the bold.
From moments of sorrow to joy's gentle touch,
In grace we find comfort, we blossom so much.

Each color a blessing, each knot a prayer,
A cloth interlaced with love's tender care.
Through trials and triumphs, we fashion our fate,
In the weaver's embrace, we resonate.

The fibers connect us, in silence we meet,
In the grace of the Father, our lives are complete.
With faith as our guide, we honor the craft,
In the dance of the sacred, we find our true path.

Beneath the starlit sky, our hearts start to sing,
In the whispers of evening, found joy in each string.
As the fabric of life wraps us tenderly tight,
In God's loving vision, our future is bright.

With each passing season, the colors do shift,
In the tapestry woven, our spirits uplift.
In the softness of grace, we're anchored and free,
Together we flourish, as one family.

In the tapestry of grace, we find unity,
In the threads of our faith, lives woven perfectly.
With love as the pattern, we shine like the sun,
In the rich tapestry, our hearts beat as one.

## Heartstrings and Higher Realms

In the depths of our being, love's melody plays,
Heartstrings connecting in mystical ways.
Each note resonates in the chambers so deep,
Awakening spirits, in reverence we weep.

With each sacred breath, our hearts start to soar,
In higher realms beckoning, we seek evermore.
In the chorus of angels, we find our sweet place,
With harmony binding, we're wrapped in His grace.

Through mountains and valleys, our souls intertwine,
In the music of prayer, His love we define.
With faith as our essence, the light leads our way,
In the dance of existence, we gather and sway.

In the garden of spirit, where dreams intertwine,
The fragrance of peace, like blossoms, divine.
With faith as our compass, our heart knows no fear,
In the song of the heavens, His whisper is clear.

As we tune to His heartbeat, our burdens release,
In the symphony grand, we embrace His sweet peace.
With every confession, each tear that we share,
In heartstrings and higher realms, His love is our air.

Together we rise, in this holy embrace,
With hearts pure and strong, we seek sacred space.
In the bond of His mercy, we find solace true,
In heartstrings and higher realms, we become anew.

## The Celestial Canvas

Upon the canvas of skies, stars twinkle so bright,
Each one a reminder of love's gentle light.
In the strokes of creation, the colors display,
The artistry of Heaven, guiding our way.

With every sunrise, a masterpiece blooms,
In the grandeur of nature, our spirit consumes.
As the sun kisses mountains, and rivers embrace,
In the beauty of moments, we find our true place.

The clouds drift above, like brush strokes at play,
In the winds of the Spirit, our worries decay.
With gratitude, we gather, in awe and in grace,
Upon the celestial canvas, we find our space.

In the twilight's soft glow, reflections ignite,
The power of creation, revealing our sight.
Each flicker of starlight, a prayer sent above,
In the heart of the cosmos, we dwell in His love.

Like artists, we flourish, in His boundless embrace,
In the gallery of life, each moment a trace.
With the Father's sweet brush, we are painted anew,
On the celestial canvas, His vision comes true.

As we stand hand in hand, gazing up at the vast,
In the wonder of darkness, we feel His love's cast.
On this canvas of life, each soul plays a part,
In the celestial dance, He captures our heart.

## **Nestled in the Embrace of Eternity**

In shadows deep where silence dwells,
A whisper stirs, a sacred spell.
The stars above, they gently glow,
In love's embrace, we find our flow.

Time rests its weary hand on grace,
In this stillness, we find our place.
The soul ignites like dawn's first light,
Nestled close, we soar in flight.

Heaven's chorus sings our names,
In unity, our spirit flames.
With every breath, we rise and bend,
To the eternal, we ascend.

Through trials faced, our faith, it binds,
In storms of life, our vision finds.
Each tear we shed, a prayer released,
In love's embrace, we find our peace.

Together we walk this holy road,
In search of truth, our hearts bestowed.
The journey long, yet never alone,
In every step, His love is known.

## Covenant of the Heart

In sacred bond, our souls entwine,
A sacred pledge, a love divine.
Each promise made, a thread of gold,
In covenant, our hearts unfold.

Through darkest nights, your hand in mine,
We rise in faith, our spirits shine.
In trials fierce, our trust will stand,
Together strong, united hand.

With every word, we truth declare,
In whispers soft, our silent prayer.
Each heartbeat sings a hymn of grace,
In love's embrace, our fears replace.

The journey etched in sacred scrolls,
In every breath, we touch our goals.
With gratitude, we share this path,
In joy, we dance, in love we bathe.

Together we forge this sacred tie,
In laughter sweet, our spirits fly.
In every moment, pure and whole,
We find our peace, we heal our soul.

## Guardian of My Roots

In the quiet earth, my lineage lies,
The whispered tales beneath the skies.
Guardian strong of ancient ways,
In humble hearts, my spirit plays.

Through shifting winds and storms that roar,
The roots hold firm, forevermore.
In every shadow, wisdom speaks,
A beacon bright, the path it seeks.

With every step, I trace my past,
In every smile, reflections cast.
The love of kin, a sacred thread,
In memories cherished, we are led.

From distant shores, their voices call,
In sacred bonds, I stand up tall.
The strength of those who walked before,
In gratitude, my spirit soars.

Through trials faced, I honor the gift,
In roots so deep, my heart will lift.
The guardian's watch, a guiding light,
In love's embrace, my future bright.

## In the Heart of the Community

In the heart of the community, we rise,
Together bound, under shared skies.
With open arms, we gather near,
In unity, we shed our fear.

Through laughter loud and stories shared,
In every soul, a love declared.
The hands that lift, the hearts that heal,
In kindness sown, our spirits feel.

In trials faced, we find our strength,
Together we journey the endless length.
With voices raised, a song of hope,
In every heart, we learn to cope.

The woven fabric of who we are,
In every thread, a shining star.
Through joy and pain, we share the light,
In love's embrace, we unite.

In the heart of the community, we stand,
With dreams and hopes, we join our hands.
In every moment, a prayer we weave,
Together strong, we shall believe.

## Echoes of Eternal Love

In the stillness of the night,
Whispers of grace take flight.
Hearts entwined in divine glow,
Love eternal, pure and slow.

In every prayer, a song resounds,
In every silence, truth abounds.
Echoes of hope through ages flow,
Binding souls, as we grow.

From mountains high to valleys deep,
In faith's embrace, our spirits leap.
Radiant light, through shadows cast,
Guiding us to love at last.

With every tear, a blessing shared,
In every laugh, the heart laid bare.
Together we rise, together we stand,
A testament to His hand.

In the twilight of our days,
We see love's unending ways.
In every moment, a chance to see,
Echoes of love, eternally free.

## The Sacred Circle of Kin

Beneath the vast and starry sky,
Hands are joined, we draw nigh.
In the circle, bonds we weave,
A tapestry of souls that believe.

Through trials faced, through joys shared,
In every heart, His love declared.
Together we journey, side by side,
In faith and trust, a sacred guide.

As seasons change and rivers flow,
We gather strength, our spirits grow.
With every story, we embrace,
The sacred circle, a holy space.

In laughter bright and tears that fall,
In shared blessings, we hear the call.
The warmth of kin, like sunlight's ray,
Guiding us on life's wondrous way.

Hearken now to love's sweet tone,
In unity, we are not alone.
Bound by grace, forever we kin,
In the sacred circle, love begins.

## **Roots in the Spirit Soil**

In the garden of the heart,
Seeds of faith we plant and start.
Nurtured by the Spirit's hand,
Roots take hold in sacred land.

Through storms that test, through winds that blow,
In the soil of love, we grow.
Branches reaching toward the light,
Guided by His grace so bright.

Each flower blooms, a story told,
In vibrant colors, love unfolds.
With every bud, a promise made,
In the Spirit's soil, never afraid.

Harvest comes, with joy we reap,
In unity, our roots run deep.
Together we stand, as one, we rise,
In the garden, beneath the skies.

From our roots, a legacy flows,
In hearts united, faith glows.
In each season, we find our role,
Trusting in the Spirit's soul.

## A Homecoming of the Soul

In the quiet of the dawn,
Whispers call, the journey's drawn.
The heart returns, its sacred quest,
To find the place where love is blessed.

Through valleys wide and mountains steep,
The soul awakes from restless sleep.
In every step, a path revealed,
In grace and mercy, wounds are healed.

The gentle breeze, a lover's sigh,
In each embrace, the heavens cry.
The light within, a guiding flame,
In homecoming, we find our name.

With open arms, the spirit waits,
In the stillness, the heart creates.
In unity, we find our peace,
In love's embrace, all struggles cease.

As dawn breaks bright, we come to know,
The truth of love's eternal flow.
In every moment, we feel the whole,
In homecoming, the joy of soul.

Printed in the USA
CPSIA information can be obtained
at www.ICGtesting.com
CBHW061044231124
17857CB00048B/588